52 Ways to Teach Missions

Easy-to-do Activities for Ages 4 -12

Author .... *Nancy S. Williamson*

Illustrators .... *Fran Kizer*
Doug Ten Napel

These pages may be copied.

Permission is granted to the buyer of this book to reproduce, duplicate or photocopy student materials in this book for use with pupils in Sunday school or Bible teaching classes.

Rainbow Publishers®

Copyright © 2003 • Fifteenth Printing
Rainbow Publishers • P.O. Box 261129 • San Diego, CA 92196
www.rainbowpublishers.com

RB36169
ISBN 0-937282-67-7

CHRIST AS A MISSIONARY

Christ was a HOME missionary in the house of Lazarus.

He was a FOREIGN missionary when the Greeks came to Him.

He was a CITY missionary when He taught in Samaria.

He was a SUNDAY SCHOOL missionary when He opened up the Word of God and set men to studying the Scriptures.

He was a CHILDREN'S missionary when He took them in His arms and blessed them.

He was a missionary to the POOR when He opened the eyes of the blind beggar.

He was a missionary to the RICH when He opened the spiritual eyes of Zacchaeus.

Even on the Cross, Christ was a missionary to the robber, and His last command was the Great Missionary Commission to us all:

"Go ye into all the world, and preach the gospel to every creature."
Mark 16:15

We can do nothing but follow His example.

Introduction

The most important activity of any church or Sunday school is to win others to Christ and then help them to grow spiritually. Christ's command to do this is strikingly explicit: "Go ye into all the world, and preach the gospel to every creature." (Mark 16:15)

Missions are not a question; they are a universal Christian obligation. Missions are not a matter of choice; they are an act of obedience to Christ.

The missionaries (and pastors and Christian workers) of tomorrow are in the Sunday school classes of today. Children are in the impressionable period of their lives; they are forming their ideals and making their life choices. For this reason, every Sunday school, every kids' club, and every youth group must present Christianity's claim of life consecration. Many, if not most, of God's servants on the mission fields and in the pulpits today committed themselves to the Lord's work before or during their teenage years.

Such service to the Lord can begin at home at a young age. Missions are simply the act of "preaching the gospel to all creatures." Home missions work includes anything that can be done to help our fellow man and show him God's love through our actions. Then, as the child grows, he can be led into missions service, as the Lord calls.

God tells us to go to the whole world. A child or teen's "whole world" probably consists of only his family, friends and neighbors. (This may also be true for many adults.) Therefore, we need to encourage our children (and all of our Sunday school members) to go forth in service on their own mission fields.

The following pages are filled with 52 exciting activities to teach the concept and importance of missions to your children and teens. (Many activities are ideal for involving the entire congregation with the children in the study of missions.)

The purpose of this book is two-fold:
1. To teach the children (and teens and adults) in your Sunday school and church so that they, personally, right in their own neighborhood, can be a missionary.
2. To enthusiastically involve the children (and every member of your congregation) in supporting missionaries and missions work through their prayers, interest, financial giving and service.

To teach about every phase of missions requires a variety of approaches. Fifty-two quick, easy and convenient ideas — one for every week of the year, if that is how you choose to use them — are provided in this book. They include games, crafts, visuals, outreach events, promotional ideas, and much more. They provide a well-rounded missions education program for your children and teens — and all age groups — in whatever type of activity or area of interest they enjoy. (Materials may also be duplicated for classroom use.)

The result: This well-rounded missions program will open the door for many spiritual blessings for your Sunday school, and for missions work at home and abroad.

52 Ways to Teach Missions

Easy-to-do Activities for Ages 4 -12

CONTENTS

1 Match His Weight Offering

OBJECTIVE: Boosts interest and involvement in missionary giving

Appropriate for ages 8 to 12 (and the entire congregation)

Choose a young man in your church who is an athlete, such as a wrestler or football player. During announcement of a special missionary outreach for which an offering is to be gathered, weigh the young man publically. Then tell the class or congregation that the goal is for the missionary offering to match the young man's weight!

Create a chart (see illustration) on which the total poundage of the offerings can be recorded from week to week.

2 TV Interviews

OBJECTIVE: Innovative way to review facts about missions and missionaries

Appropriate for ages 10 to 13

Plan a special TV interview as a way to get your students excited about missionary facts.

Make a simple "television set" from a large cardboard box. Remove the top, and cut the bottom out of a box, leaving a frame about 3 inches wide. Place the box on its side on a covered table with the bottom facing the audience. The child appearing on TV stands behind the table so he is seen through the hole in the box. Other students ask him questions about missions and missionaries until he answers a question incorrectly.

Another idea:

One student pretends to be a missionary and reports his activities. Or two students may appear on "screen" together, with one acting as a reporter and the other the missionary.

3 Missionaries' Names

OBJECTIVE: Ideas to help your students learn missionaries' names

Appropriate for ages 6 to 12

Make a mini-poster about 3 by 10 inches in size and paste on a picture of a missionary and write on his or her name. Attach a string to the mini-poster and hang a poster around each child's neck. He or she will be called by the missionary's name during the missions' emphasis period or class session. Tell the class (or let each student tell the class) about the missionary, where they serve and what they do, etc.

Other ideas:

* Here's how to make a game which always captures the interest of children: After you have talked about several missionaries and shown their pictures to the class, post a photo, the name of each missionary, where they serve and, if desired, a short biography about each missionary on the wall.
  Safety pin a mini-poster to each child's back. The children move about the room asking each other yes or no questions until they determine which missionary they are. First one to do so is the winner.
* Make flash cards of missionaries' pictures with flannel on the back. Make other flannel-backed flash cards of the missionaries' names

and/or of their mission field, occupation (doctor, nurse, teacher, pastor, etc.). Students enjoy matching the missionaries' pictures with the appropriate names and information on the flannel board.

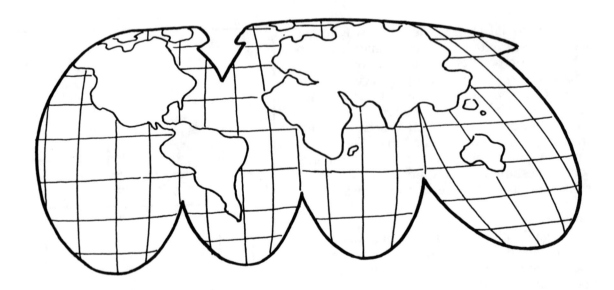

4 Adopt A Missionary

OBJECTIVE: Introduces children to a missionary child they can be friends with

Appropriate for age 6 to teens

Have your class "adopt" a missionary child who is approximately their age. Names and pictures of missionary families should be available from your denomination.

Here are some ways your class can get better acquainted with their missionary child and do some very special "surprise kindnesses" for him or her:

- Write individual or group letters or record cassette tapes to the missionary child. The children in your class can tell things about themselves—how old they are, what grade they are in, what they are studying in Sunday school, and facts about themselves and their families.

Suggest that your class ask the missionary child questions about himself, the place where he lives, and ways he and his family tell people about Jesus. They can also tell the child they are praying for him, and ask for his prayer requests.

- Your class can send copies of their take-home papers to the missionary child each month or quarter. Children can take turns saving their papers to bring back for mailing.
- Send birthday, Christmas and other greeting cards or gifts to the missionary child throughout the year. Keep in mind the time needed for the cards or gifts to arrive on the mission field and mail in plenty of time.
- Send Christian children's books, or stories on cassette tapes.
- Send pictures of the children in your class to the missionary child. Ask for him or her to send your class a picture and write back. Mount the picture and letter in your classroom.
- In July, have each child bring a special Christmas gift to send to their missionary child. (Also see "Another idea" in "Christmas in July" on page 31)
- Don't forget the siblings of your missionary

child. If possible, ask other classes to adopt the siblings and use these ideas. If this is not possible, try to include some special letters or gifts for the siblings in each package sent.

- When the family of your adopted missionary child comes home on furlow or for deputation work, try to set up a speaking engagement at your church so your class has the opportunity to meet their special adopted missionary "brother" or "sister."

Other ideas:

- Adopt a child in a missionary orphanage or hospital and carry out many of the same kindnesses for him or her.
- Your women's missionary group could adopt a needy woman on the mission field, (perhaps a widow with several children recommended by the local missionaries) and do special kindnesses for her.

5 Fishers Of Men Picture

OBJECTIVE: Presents Peter as a Bible missionary; aids memorization

Appropriate for ages 5 to 9

Tell the story of Peter to the class, summarizing his life story (fisherman, one of Jesus' disciples, betrayed Jesus, repented, became outspoken missionary, his preaching brought 3000 people into the church in one day, made several missionary trips to tell others about Jesus). He became a missionary because he loved the Lord and wanted everyone else to know about Him.

Review some of the things Peter did to follow the Lord and tell others about Him. Discuss the Scripture, "Follow Me, and I will make you fishers of men." (Matthew 4:19)

Be sure the children understand that being fishers of men means to tell others about Jesus. This is what missionaries do and this is what Peter did. Explain that the children can be missionaries too, by telling other people about Jesus.

Duplicate for each child the Fishers of Men Picture activity sheet from page 11 and distribute. Give the children time to color the picture. Then give each child a hair net or a piece of nylon net to glue to the side of the boat to form a "fishing net", (see illustration). (Be sure to glue the netting into a pocket shape so it will hold the paper memory verse fish below.)

Keep the picture in class for a few weeks. Each week, type or write out the memory verse on a small piece of construction paper and cut into the shape of a fish. (Pattern below) Make one each

week for each child. When each child has learned the verse, he may put the fish into the fishing net.

After the unit is complete, each child may take his picture home to remind him to be a fisher of men.

Suggested Scriptures:
Matthew 4:19; Mark 16:15

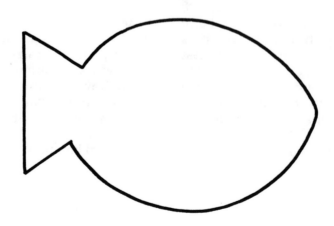

FISHERS OF MEN PICTURE

Color the picture. Then glue a hair net or piece of net to the side of the boat to make a fishing net. You will be given a fish to put in the net each week you learn your memory verse.

(Jesus said), "Follow Me, and I will make you fishers of men."
Matthew 4:19

6 Progressive Dinner

OBJECTIVE: Acquaints participants with missions information in fun settings

Appropriate for age 10 to teens (and the entire congregation)

Older children, teens and adults enjoy progressive dinners. Here's the way to combine the fun of progressive dinners with the adventure of sampling foreign foods, while celebrating and supporting missions.

Each home in the progressive dinner should be decorated to represent a different country and feature foods from that country. Prepare place cards at each home telling missions information about the country represented. During or before dinner, the guests can read the cards aloud and share information about missions in that nation. Music, dramatic skits, or readings about the nation being studied could also be included.

A short profile of a missionary from each country can be presented at the different homes, and before leaving each home, the entire group should pause to pray for the needs and missionaries in that particular country. Small business-size cards, with the missionaries name and pertinent missions facts or prayer requests, could be given to each guest.

Another idea:

This progressive dinner could also be organized as a missions fund-raiser with guests making a contribution to missions at each home, or paying a "ticket" price for the entire dinner.

7 Map Identification

OBJECTIVE: Colorful reminder of missionaries' service around the world

Appropriate for ages 8 to teens (and the entire congregation)

Cover a bulletin board with a large map of the world, and mount photos of missionaries around the edges. (Be sure to accompany the photos with the name(s) and locations of the missionaires pictured.) Include one of the Suggested Scriptures below on the bulletin board either by cutting letters from black construction paper, or write the verse directly on the map using a wide felt-tip marker.

Run string, yarn or ribbon from the pictures to the countries where the missionaries serve. Short biographies of the missionaries could be included beside the photos. Alternatively, you could cluster the missionaries' pictures around the area of the world they represent.

Contact your denominational missions department for photos of your missionaries, or offer your missionaries free film, developing, and postage of photos they take on the field.

This is an outstanding display for a busy area of your church, such as the entrance lobby or fellowship hall.

Other ideas:

- To demonstrate the wide variety of work done by missionaries, and the many places around the world to which they are called to serve, make a collage by collecting pictures of the missionaries, their places of work (such as hospitals and schools), and the native peoples to whom they minister. Arrange these on a large bulletin board or bordering a map. See illustration below.

- For a bulletin board for younger children, place pictures of the children of missionaries on a map. Listing the names, ages and birthdays of the missionary kids will help your students relate to them, pray for them and realize that not only adults, but also children, are serving Jesus on the mission field. See illustration below.

Suggested Scriptures:
Mark 16:15; Acts 1:8; Psalm 2:8

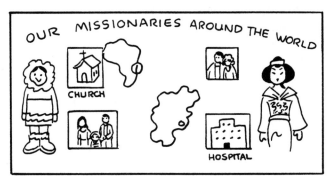

8 Foreign Words

OBJECTIVE: Teaches children the words to Christian songs in foreign languages

Appropriate for age 6 to teens

It's fun to learn some simple foreign phrases, Scriptures and songs. To accompany lessons on missions, teach your class to say or sing a popular Scripture or song in the language of the mission field being studied.

To reinforce the great diversity of languages around the world (and the difficulties of learning some languages), display some translations of Scriptures in different languages on a table or bulletin board. (Contact the American Bible Society, P.O. Box 5636, Grand Central Station, New York, NY 10164, for a listing of Scripture translations available.) Talk about what must be done to translate the Bible into a new language.

Here are some easy-to-learn translations of two popular Christian children's songs your class is sure to enjoy learning:

Jesus Loves the Little Children
English:
>   Jesus loves the little children,
>   All the children of the world.
>   Red or yellow, black or white,
>   We are precious in His sight.
>   Jesus loves the little children of the world.

French:
>   Jesu aime les enfants,
>   Tous les enfants du monde.
>   Rouge et jaune, noir et blanc,
>   Ils sont precioux dans sa vision.
>   Jesu aime les enfants du monde.

Spanish:
>   Cristo ama a los ninos,
>   Cuantos en el mundo estan.
>   No le importa tu color,
>   A Jesus el Salvador.
>   Cristo ama a los ninos por doquier.

Jesus Loves Me
English:
>   Yes, Jesus loves me.
>   Yes, Jesus loves me.
>   Yes, Jesus loves me.
>   The Bible tells me so.

Spanish:
>   Si, Cristo me ama.
>   Si, Cristo me ama.
>   Si, Cristo me ama.
>   La Biblia dice asi.

Japanese:
>   Wa ga Shu ie-su.
>   Wa ga Shu ie-su.
>   Wa ga Shu ie-su.
>   Wa re o a i su.

German:
>   Ja, Jesus liebt mich.
>   Ja, Jesus liebt mich.
>   Ja, Jesus liebt mich.
>   Die Bibel sagt mir dies.

9 Missionary Me

Appropriate for age 10 to teens (and the entire congregation)

Jesus has commanded all of us to "Go . . . into all the world, and preach the gospel to every creature." (Mark 16:15). Jesus did not call just the missionaries or full-time Christian workers; He called us too, and we have just as much obligation to obey His command.

Here are some simple, easy ways any Christian can be a missionary right in his own neighborhood. None require special skills or abilities or finances. All that's needed is love for the Lord and a desire to obey Him by sharing the Gospel with others:

- Be prepared to share the message of salvation and lead someone to accept Jesus as their personal Savior.
- Give parties for crippled or disabled children.
- Help a needy or elderly person fix up their house or clean their yard.
- Volunteer to drive disabled or elderly persons shopping or to appointments.
- Personally deliver the Sunday school paper to those who missed class.
- Conduct services at nursing homes, or simply visit a nursing home and offer to read to residents, write letters for them, or help in other ways.
- Provide a tape ministry for shut-ins by delivering a tape of the Sunday worship service or other Christian music or messages.
- Make daily telephone calls to check on elderly or disabled persons who live alone.
- Run errands for shut-ins.
- Look around your church and community for

other ways you can spread the Gospel and other areas of need that can be filled by you: a true home missionary!

Another idea:

Emphasize to your congregation that we are all missionaries no matter where we live and work. Provide copies (perhaps in the church bulletin) of the list above and other specific needs in your church and ask for volunteers to take on these ministries. Have a coordinator ready to organize the volunteers who are sure to respond.

10 World Time Chart

OBJECTIVE: Aids effective prayer for missions

Appropriate for ages 9 to 12

This World Time Chart is a wonderful teaching tool for all ages. As we get ready to pray for our missionaries, we can look at the chart and see what time of day or night it is where they are and have some idea of what they might be doing at that particular time.

Duplicate the circles on page 17 for each student. Prior to class, glue each circle onto tagboard or lightweight cardboard and allow to dry. (If you have access to a copy machine which can copy onto lightweight card stock, you can elminate the need to glue the circles to tagboard.) Punch a hole in the center of each circle.

In class, give each child one of each of the circles. Give the children time to cut them out and color them, if desired. Show the children how to put their wheel together, (see illustration) with the smaller circle on top, and fasten with a paper fastener. Tape down the prongs of the paper fastener to prevent scratching.

Show the children how to use their World Time Chart. Turn the smaller circle to the time of day or night it is where you live. On the outside ring, find the country where the missionary lives. Look at the corresponding time on the smaller circle to see what time it is where the missionary lives.

To be sure the children understand how to use the wheel ask them several questions:

When you are eating lunch, what time is it in Australia? (For North America, between 3 and 6 a.m.)

When boys and girls in India are eating lunch, where are you? (In bed)

When it is 8 p.m. in Israel, where are you likely to be on a weekday? (School)

Encourage the children to use their charts to pray for the missionaries several times throughout the day and to think about what the missionaries are doing at that time.

To help the children know what to pray for, talk about what some of the missionaries needs

might be at a specific time of the day. For example:

Nightime	Safety
Daytime	God's help with work
Evening	God's rest and peace
Lunch	Blessing of food to body
Breakfast	Strength for new day

A good verse to remember when thinking about praying for others all around the world is Psalm 145:18. Help the children memorize this verse which is on their World Time Charts.

Another idea:

• Using a copy machine with enlarging capabilites, enlarge the two circles to make a giant prayer wheel for use in the classroom. Each week during class, ask one child to use the wheel to see what time of day it is in a different county and what the missionaries might be doing. Then pray for those missionaries.

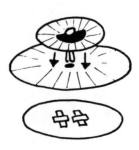

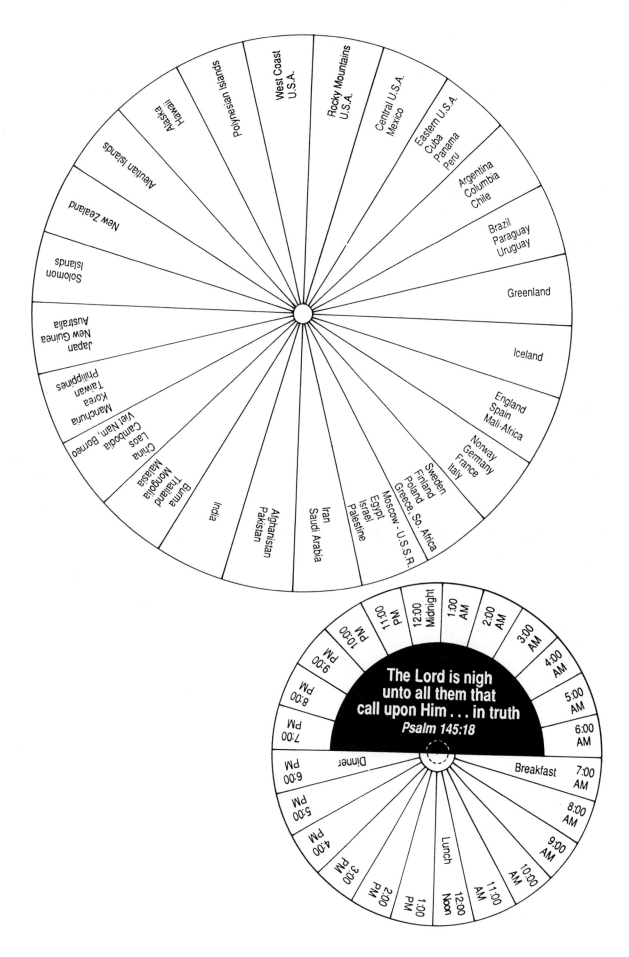

The Lord is nigh unto all them that call upon Him . . . in truth
Psalm 145:18

11 Missions Resource Files

OBJECTIVE: Exciting ways to keep your class thinking about missions

Appropriate for ages 6 to 12

Children enjoy collecting all sorts of things. Capitalize on this by asking them to help you collect pictures, articles, and other information on the various areas of the world in which your church supports mission work.

First, introduce the idea of the resource file to your class. Then post a list of mission fields and missionaries at some prominent spot in your room. Ask the children to bring in clippings, pictures, books and objects telling about the countries or from the countries.

Store the materials, by country or mission field name in a file cabinet or large cardboard box in your classroom.

A three-ring, loose-leaf notebook may be used instead of file folders (and will probably be more effective in encouraging students to look through the materials in spare moments). Use colored paper or colored tabs to create category divisions within the books, such as: "the people," "customs," "the land," "today's happenings," "home and dress," "schools," and "our missionaries."

Sources of material and information for your resource file:

- missionary newsletters and magazines
- denominational headquarters
- encyclopedias
- postcards
- travel folders
- magazines and newspapers
- radio and television programs

Some students may also find informational tidbits from their social studies work at school.

Other ideas:

- Always give the students time to share with the class what they have learned or brought to the class before it is added to the resource file.
- As the children develop the resource file, they will learn of the people, needs and conditions

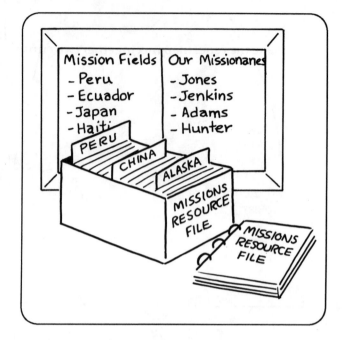

on the mission fields. The habit of praying for our missionaries can be developed by encouraging the students to set up a special "prayer request" bulletin board in the classroom showing various mission fields and their needs. Each week, have one child lead in prayer for these missions' needs.

- Devote a short part (5 to 7 minutes) of each Sunday school class or club night meeting to missions. Each week one child can share some interesting information about one of the mission fields or show and tell about his contribution to the resource file. Children can be asked in advance to tell a missionary story to the class, to learn about one specific aspect of missionary life and share it with the class, or to "introduce" the class to one missionary family (preferrably a family with children about the age of your class).

12 ⬚ Relief Map Making

OBJECTIVE: Map study teaches about mission fields, people and places

Appropriate for ages 8 to 12

Children will enjoy making this relief map which shows the topography of the country being studied.

To make the relief map mix together two cups of salt and one cup of flour. Add enough water to make a stiff paste.

Draw the outline of the country on heavy cardboard or a piece of masonite or plywood. Spread the salt and flour mixture over the map outline. Build up hills and mountains, carve out lakes and rivers using a nail file or spoon and form other topographical features as desired.

When the mixture has dried thoroughly, the relief map can be painted with tempera paints or acrylics.

In the meantime, the children will have fun making a table-top village to go beside the map showing a typical village in the country displayed in the relief map. (The map could also be made large enough to allow room to build a tiny village right on the map.)

While the children work, tell them about the nation and its people, the climate and crops, and point out where the country is on a globe or world map. (Use information you have collected in the Missions Resource Files activity on page 18.) Also tell about the missionaries at work there. If a picture of a real village where one of your missionaries serves is available, the children will enjoy following the picture in creating their village.

Most houses and buildings can be made from small boxes and construction paper. (Be sure to include the church or mission compound in the village.) Clothespin dolls or figures made from pipe cleaners or chenille wire can be dressed according to the customs of the country using

scraps of fabric or construction paper glued into place.

Tiny cooking pots, rocks and other items can be formed with modeling clay or salt and floor mixture. Bits of grass or a thin layer of sand can be glued to a piece of cardboard to serve as the base for the entire village. Use aluminum foil to simulate water, and make trees by sticking small twigs into bits of clay to make them stand up. Glue everything in place onto the base and add a placard naming the place and country in which this village might be found.

This is an attractive display for the church entrance lobby or fellowship hall prior to the visit of a missionary from that nation.

13 | Mission Dioramas

OBJECTIVE: Introduces children to the missionaries and people of foreign lands

Appropriate for ages 8 to 12

Each child will construct a simple scene showing life in a foreign nation, and write a short article about their nation.

Allow each child to choose the nation he wishes to study. (Allow choices from only those nations where there are mission fields and missionaries your church supports.) Be sure you have enough information on each nation in your Mission Resource File (see page 18) or from other sources.

Children may write a short article about the missionaries or country they chose. (Suggest to the children that they do the research for their article before beginning their diorama; this will help them make their diorama more authentic and accurate.) When complete, mount each article on construction paper cut out in the shape of the outline of the country and display on a bulletin board behind the diorama.

Before beginning construction of the dioramas, collect pictures of foreign countries and peoples from missions magazines, National Geographic magazines, postcards or travel folders. Have each student bring in a shoe box with cover. (Be sure to have some extra boxes for the children who forget to bring one.)

Lay the box on its side and place the cover beneath the box so the cover protrudes to give an extended space for the scene. Staple or glue into place. (See illustration.) The outside of the shoe box may be covered with construction paper or Contact.

Plan the scene first, allowing enough room for the magazine photos. Be careful to space the various elements for proper three-dimensional effects. (It is usually best to limit the diorama to three main elements, i.e. a person, a house and a tree, plus the background which is glued to the bottom (back of the scene) and ends (sides of the

scene) of the shoe box.

Paste on fringed green construction paper for grass, and blue paper for the sky. Glue on fluffy cotton ball clouds and cut out tiny flying birds. To make a lake or pond, draw small fish on blue construction paper and cover with Saran Wrap. Make purple mountains in the distance, and dark green hills with small twig trees. Spread glue or paste for a path or roadway and cover with sand, dirt, rocks or pebbles.

Make people and animals of pipe cleaners or chenille wire, construction paper, clothespins or clay. Glue into place.

To make the photograph element stand away from the walls of the diorama, glue the photo to lightweight cardboard. When dry, cut out leaving a tab at the bottom to fold back and glue to the base of the diorama.

14 Poster Contest

OBJECTIVE: Involve children in creatively thinking about missions

Appropriate for age 8 to teens

Announce a poster contest involving missions. Choose a theme related to missions—praying, giving, going, God's call, etc., or use your denomination's yearly missionary theme.

Standard size of the posters should be approximately 14 by 20 inches; wording should be no longer than ten words. Illustrations may be made by cutting and pasting letters or shapes to the poster board, or by drawing directly onto the poster board. Set a date by which all entries must be received, and publicize the awards which will be given. (Offer an appropriate first, second and third place award in each age category.)

Display the posters around the church and provide ballots for voting on the winners. Or select three judges from the congregation to choose the winners. After the winners are declared, attach award ribbons and leave the posters on display as a reminder to the entire congregation of the importance of missions.

Other ideas:

• This poster contest could also be carried out on a district or presbytery level with winners from each church competing with each other for a grand prize. The prize might be an item from a mission field.

• Develop an essay contest along these same guidelines. Determine a subject and length of the essay. Some suggested topics are: "What is a missionary?" "How I can be a missionary now," or "What Jesus showed us about how to be a missionary."

15

After The Missionaries Came

OBJECTIVE: Dramatically shows the importance of missionary work

Appropriate for age 8 to teens (and the entire congregation)

These character sketches, which can be preformed by children or teens, clearly show what are the far-reaching effects of missionary work. Use these character sketches as part of a missions program or as part of a missions lesson in your classroom.

For public performance, give the performers their parts to learn and meet with them for practice. (For presentation in your classroom, the performers can read their parts.) Dress the players in clothing representing their country.

AFRICA

My home is in Africa, across the ocean. Before the missionaries came and told me about Jesus, I was afraid of evil spirits. I made statues of them with stones and sticks and feathers. I bowed down and worshiped these statues. Sometimes when I was very hungry my parents took the only food in the house and gave it to these statues so the evil spirits would not harm us. Now I know that Jesus is more powerful than any evil spirits, anywhere. I have asked the Lord Jesus to make me a part of God's family. Now I worship Him.

SOUTH AMERICA

My home is in South America. I live in a small village. Before the missionaries came and told me about Jesus, I thought there were many gods. I was afraid of these gods and I was afraid of evil spirits. Our village had a special gate people had to enter so the evil spirits wouldn't be able to come into the village with them. Now I know there is only one God. I know God loves me and does not want me to be afraid of Him. I have asked Jesus to make me a part of God's family. The missionaries are translating the books of the Bible into my language. Soon I will be able to read about Jesus in the Bible. I am happy because I have Jesus, and I know God loves me.

INDIA

My home is in India. Before the missionaries came and told me about Jesus I worshipped bugs! Yes, bugs! I was taught that when people die they come back to earth again in some other form. That form might even be a bug. I would never kill an ant or swat a fly. I thought that a fly or ant might be my grandmother who died. Sometimes we would be very hungry, but we would never kill a chicken or a cow to eat. We thought these might be someone who died and came back to earth as an animal. But now I have asked Jesus to make me a part of God's family. I know that dead people do not come back to life as bugs or cows. I know that when I die I will go to heaven to live with Jesus.

CHINA

My home is in China. Before the missionaries came and told me about Jesus I worshipped my ancestors. Ancestors are people in your family who died long ago, like great grandfathers and great uncles. Our family had an altar in the house. We had household gods and wooden tablets with a list of all our ancestors on them. My father burned incense to show reverence for the gods. The roof of our house is pointed up on the ends so that evil spirits landing on it will slide right back up into the sky. I am glad the missionaries came and told me about Jesus. I have invited Him to make me a part of God's family. I know that God wants us to worship Him only. He wants everybody to know and love Him. I have learned that I do not need to fear evil spirits because Jesus has the power to keep me safe.

AMERICA

My home is in America. I always *thought* I was a Christian because I lived in America. Then a minister came to our house and told me the only way to become a Christian was by inviting Jesus to make me a part of God's family. So that is what I did. Now I *know* that I am a Christian. When Jesus came into my life He gave me the strength to live a good life. He gives me the strength to obey my parents and to do my school work well. When I have a problem I can go to Him with it in prayer and He helps me with it. I am glad the minister came to tell me about Jesus. Now I go to Sunday school each week.

Other ideas:
- Parts needn't be memorized perfectly. Performers can ad-lib a bit, with practice. Make sure they cover all the important points in the sketch.
- If desired, tape record the five sketches before the presentation and simply play back the tape during the presentation. This eliminates the need for the performers to memorize their parts.
- Children love puppets and they can help teach missions in a way that will hold interest. Use simple puppets to give these character sketches. Simply use a piece of fabric, or hat to indicate country. For example; in the African sketch, shroud the puppet in a piece of leopard-skin printed fabric.

Puppets can also be used for other missions teachings: The puppets can give information about each of the mission areas you are studying as they travel from country to country in native dress. They can also help teach foreign phrases, Scriptures and songs.

16 Crib Quilt

OBJECTIVE: Creates a beautiful gift for a missionary child on the mission field

Appropriate for ages 5 to 10

Select a missionary couple who are expecting a baby or have a new baby, or select an orphanage for which the quilt can be made. Each child in your class will make a special quilt block which will be sewn together with the others to form a crib quilt.

Give each child one 8-inch square of un-bleached muslin. Ask the children to draw a very special picture directly onto the fabric using crayons. (Color heavily for best results.) They should also include their name. (Talk to the children about the missionary family or the orphanage that is to be recepient of the quilt to help them choose pictures to draw onto their quilt blocks. You might suggest they draw pictures of favorite toys or animals which the baby or child may not have in another country. Or each child could do one or two of the ABC's with a drawing of an animal or object which begins with that letter.)

After the block has been completed, the teacher or another adult should place it between two pieces of brown paper and press with a medium-hot iron to set the crayon. An adult should sew the blocks together, sew on a flannel backing and bind the edges. Tack the corners of each block with pretty yarn. Upon completion, send the quilt to the mission field accompanied by a note (and a Polaroid photograph, if possible) of your class.

Another idea:

Choose a missionary child who is about the same age as your students. He or she will be the recepient of this Love Quilt:

Buy a light-colored bedspread or piece of pre-quilted fabric (bind the edges). Give each child a sheet of white paper and fabric crayons (obtained from a craft store) and ask them to draw their favorite pet or scene on the white paper using the fabric crayons. Advise the children to keep the

picture very simple and color darkly for best results.

Have each child also write his name on a separate sheet of paper, then help the children trace their names BACKWARDS below their drawing so it will appear correctly on the quilt.

The teacher or another adult should artistically position the drawings on the quilt, and add this special message, written backwards: "To (child's name) with love, (sign your class name and/or church)." Additional words can be added if desired.

Iron the pictures, names and words onto the bedspread following the directions provided with the fabric crayons.

When the quilt is finished, mail it to the missionary child along with personal letters (and a photo, if possible) from your class telling what they do at home, church and school.

17 Missions Club

OBJECTIVE: Ensures continual emphasis on missions among members of all ages

Appropriate for age 6 to teens (and the entire congregation)

The establishment of a missions club ensures continual missions awareness and support among your entire congregation.

Many churches already have a women's missionary society, but why not consider some additional groups like these?

- A group for children held once a week after school or on Wednesday night
- A group for men meeting at a prayer breakfast once a week, perhaps on Saturday morning
- A teen group
- A mother's morning out group

Use these clubs as an opportunity to teach the members about the mission fields and their needs, and to make the members a part of actively supporting the missionaries in prayer, service, and giving. Involve the club members in practical missions service, either in "home missions" activities (ministering to the homeless, abused women, needy, shuts-ins, etc.) or in raising funds and support for foreign missionaries. Members can also do practical service around the church: children and teens can rake leaves, sweep, vacuum, help in the church office and much more.

Use the ideas in this book for developing activities and outreaches, and write your denominational headquarters for current outreaches.

One church's experience proves the powerful impact a missions club can have: In order to encourage teens to get involved in missions work, this church organized a "recruit group" of high school juniors and seniors. They meet at the church at 6 a.m. each Saturday for coffee, doughnuts, prayer, study and work.

As part of their club activities, this recruit group plans and prepares a missions exhibit for the church foyer each month and researches various needs on the mission fields for which teens (and other groups within the church) raise funds. The teens also maintain regular contact with several missionaries to offer them encouragement and prayer for their work on the mission field.

The result is that the teens are vitally involved, interested and concerned with missions around the world, and hopefully several will answer the call of the Lord to the mission field!

There is no better reason for a club than this!

18 | Missions Giving Scale

OBJECTIVE: Promotes giving to missions

Appropriate for age 6 to teens

Present to the children a missions project for which they are asked to give. The boys will compete against the girls to see who can bring the offering which weighs the most. In addition, to prevent offerings of virtually nothing but pennies, the boys and girls will also compete to see who brings the largest offering.

Build a scale offering container as shown in the diagram. Each week the children bring their missions offering and place it in the appropriate bucket. Be prepared for some lively competition as the class waits to see which offering bucket tips the scale most. Then count the offering. Give one point to the team bringing the heaviest offering and one point to the team bringing the largest offering. At the end of the contest (usually four to six weeks in duration), the winning side could host the losers in a party.

A regular bathroom scale can be substituted to weigh the donations.

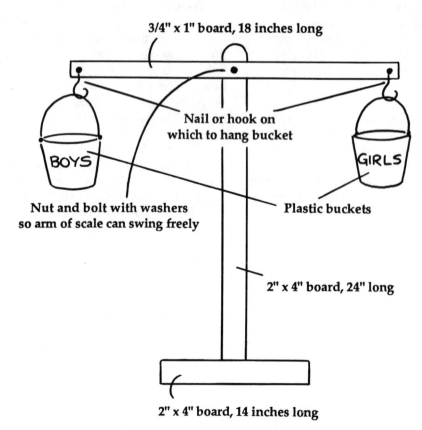

3/4" x 1" board, 18 inches long

Nail or hook on which to hang bucket

Nut and bolt with washers so arm of scale can swing freely

Plastic buckets

2" x 4" board, 24" long

2" x 4" board, 14 inches long

19 Teaching With Food

OBJECTIVE: Delicious ways to be sure your missions lessons are remembered

Appropriate for ages 6 to 12

When studying about different countries, involve the senses of taste and smell in the learning by serving ethnic food along with the lesson. Here are some suggestions:

In studying Japan, prepare sukiyaki in an electric skillet or on a hibachi right at the table. Eat with chopsticks and follow the Japanese custom of removing your shoes and sitting on the floor to eat.

If you're studying the Polynesian Islands, plan a luau, complete with a pig on a spit and dishes made with pineappple.

Remember, each country has its own distinct food and dining customs. Including them in your study will help your class understand and remember people of various countries much better.

20 Pantomime

OBJECTIVE: Reinforces what a missionary does

Appropriate for ages 6 to 12

To review with the children what activities a missionary does, have several children pantomime (act out) activities carried out by a missionary which they learned about.

The rest of the class tries to identify the name of the missionary, the country or the activity being acted out.

Use this activity as a way to teach and review exactly what a missionary does. For example; a missionary doctor may actually preach, treat patients, oversee staff, etc., and have a far wider range of activities than a United States doctor.

Another good application of this activity is to see how much the children remember of a presentation by a visiting missionary who told about his or her activities.

Appropriate for ages 5 to 11

Make one large pinata for the entire class or make smaller ones so that each member can have his own as you study about Latin American missions.

Following are instructions for making the pinata:

Cut crepe paper strips two-inches wide across the grain, cutting thought the entire folded package of crepe paper. Dip in liquid starch. (Unfold one end of the strip before dipping in the starch or the paper will stick together and it will be hard to find the end.) Allow to soak just long enough for the starch to soak through the entire fold. Squeeze out the excess starch and carefully wrap the strip around an inflated balloon. Cover the balloon evenly with three or four layers of paper. Leave a small opening at the neck of the balloon.

The size and shape of the pinata will depend upon the size and shape of your balloon. You may use one large balloon or two smaller balloons. A very interesting effect can be achieved by putting several shapes together. For example, use a sausage-shaped balloon for a body and a small, round one for the head. Each balloon can be covered individually and when dried the two shapes can be glued together. Or have a helper hold the two balloons together while you wrap strips of crepe paper to bind the two balloons together.

After the balloons are wrapped, hang to dry overnight. When dry, deflate and remove the balloons.

Fill the pinata with small wrapped candies, inexpensive toys and party favors. Type or write out portions for your missions lesson on slips of note paper, roll and tie with yarn or ribbon. Add these to the candy and toys in the pinata.

After the pinata is filled, glue the parts together (if you have more than one separate balloon) and add face markings with a felt-tip pen.

Close the top opening with more wet crepe paper and allow to dry. With an ice pick, poke two small holes in the top of the pinata. Thread a 12-15 inch wire through the holes and hang the pinata from the ceiling.

Make a "bat" from the cardboard tube from a roll of wrapping paper. Decorate the tube with strips of crepe paper wound spiral-fashion around it. (A plastic baseball bat could be used instead.)

When you are ready to present the lesson, blindfold the students one at a time and give each a turn at trying to break the pinata with the bat. When someone succeeds in breaking the pinata, all the children may scramble for the candy and surprises. After calm is restored, the children who picked up the lesson portions are asked to read them. (The lesson portions can be numbered if they should be read in sequence.)

22 | Mile Of Nickels

OBJECTIVE: Gets the entire church involved in giving for missions

Appropriate for age 6 to teens (and the entire church congregation)

Sometimes its hard to get an entire department or even the entire congregation, interested and involved in giving for a specific missions outreach. Here's an innovative way that's practically guaranteed to pique everyone's interest AND participation.

You will need ribbon, the more the better, so we suggest heavy gift wrap ribbon approximately 1/2 to 3/4 inch wide. (The ribbon needs to be heavy enough to support the weight of the nickels.)

Cut the ribbon in one yard lengths and distribute one or two yards to each class. (It would be well for you to briefly explain the "Mile of Nickels" to the class at this time.)

Each Sunday as the nickels are brought in for this missionary offering, each class is to tape their nickels to their piece of ribbon, placing the nickels side by side along the length of the ribbon. (It's wise to put a piece of tape across the nickels perpendicular to the length of the ribbon.) As each yard of ribbon is filled with nickels, the class is to begin a new piece. Collect the completed yards each week.

On the final Sunday of this emphasis, safety pin all the ribbons from all the classes together. Then, during a special assembly or during the worship service, unroll your mile of nickels, having one or two people hold the ribbon at yard intervals. Depending on the "length" of your collection, you might have to line up around the walls of the auditorium or sanctuary in order to

have room for your nickel-filled ribbon.

Since this is a good activity for all ages, quarters could be used instead of nickels. This is also an excellent opportunity to get lots of publicity for your church. Take pictures and send them to your denomination headquarters for publication in the missions magazine. (And be sure to include a copy in your next "News and Notes" mailing. See page 30.) Your local newspaper might be interested in this unusual story too.

Here is what your offering will total: (There are 5280 feet in one mile.)

1 foot of nickels	14 nickels	70¢
1 yard of nickels	42 nickels	$2.10
50 yards of nickels (150 feet)	2,100 nickels	$105.00
100 yards of nickels (300 feet)	4,200 nickels	$210.00
1 mile of nickels (1,760 yards)	73,920 nickels	$3,696.00

Your mile of nickels will weigh approximately 925 pounds!

23 [News And Notes]

OBJECTIVE: Keeps missionaries informed and feeling part of your church family

Appropriate for age 6 to teens (and the entire congregation)

Your missionaries are just like you — they enjoy reading about church happenings and people they know. They are always happy to receive newspaper clippings, church newsletters, and news of interesting events.

Decorate an "event collection box" and place it in a prominent place in the church where children, or the entire congregation can deposit newspaper clippings, pictures and even personal notes to the missionaries your local church supports.

Cover the box with colorful paper, glue on some snapshots and newspaper clippings and label the box "News and Notes for the _____ (name of the missionary family)." Add a placard stating the purpose of the box and encouraging the entire church family to participate by contributing their special news. You might also want to announce this in the church bulletin or from the pulpit.

Designate one person to gather the items every few weeks and send them to the missionaries.

Another idea:

• Encourage every family to contribute their annual Christmas letter to the "event collection box."

24 Christmas In July

OBJECTIVE: Share Christmas joy with God's servants on the mission field

Appropriate for ages 6 to 12 (and the entire congregation)

Christmas is one of the most important times of the year to remember our missionaries since they must be away from home and many of their loved ones. This gives us opportunity to reach out to them with the love God gave to us when He sent His precious Son to be born.

In order to collect items to send to the mission field in time for them to arrive by Christmas, plans must begin early in the year.

Put up a decorated Christmas tree, in a prominent part of the church, in July and ask everyone to bring gift items which can be sent to the missionaries to hang on the tree or place beneath the tree. It's a good idea to have a prepared listing of needed gift items. Play Christmas music to help set the mood for giving.

Be sure to check with the local post office to see when packages to the mission stations must be mailed for receipt by Christmas. Also find out about special forms to be filled out or other regulations you should be aware of before sending the packages.

Another idea:

Another great idea for the Christmas in July event, and one which is effective for use with children, is to make a Missionary Child's Shoebag.

Choose one missionary kid (or a missionary family with one or more children). Buy a shoebag with several separate compartments. Ask each student in your class to bring gifts for the missionary child to be put in each of the shoebag compartments. Missionary children love the same things your students love for gifts–balls, clay, balloons, dolls, books, models and craft kits, art materials, etc.

When the bag is filled with wrapped gifts in each compartment, it can be sent to the missionary child. What an exciting gift to receive when you are far away at Christmas!

(Your students could also be encouraged to send a picture of themselves and/or write a short note telling about themselves to accompany their gift.)

Appropriate for ages 5 to 10

These imaginary tours to countries around the world are an excellent way to make missions real to young children. Try to schedule one imaginary flight to a different nation each week for several weeks. At the end of the unit, review what the children have learned by playing one of the fun "review" games in this book. (Who Am I? page 37; Pantomime, page 27; TV Interviews, page 7; Missionaries' Names, page 8)

Take a picture of each child with an instant camera using either black and white or color film. (Or photograph each child a week or so before this class and have the photos developed.)

Duplicate the passport on page 33 onto blue construction paper for each child. Paste the child's picture into the passport, and below the photo print the child's name. (If desired, you could print the child's age, height, weight, etc.) Give each child his or her passport.

Then you're all ready to begin the imaginary flight to a country being studied. It's best to limit each tour to one country per week so the children have an opportunity to really learn about each individual nation.

Prepare the room to look like the interior of a 747 with seats in rows, with aisles, etc. There will be a pilot (the leader) and flight attendants (assistants, played by older children or teens) to help with the program. A screen at the front of the room (like used for in-flight movies) could be used to show slides of the country to be visited on the trip, and background music adds to the atmosphere.

Start the imaginary flight by posing as the airplane pilot as you "take off." You may even pretend to encounter some "turbulence" while in flight, so give the usual airline announcements such as; "be sure to keep your seat belts fastened" and "keep seats in the upright position."

You (the pilot) and your assistants (flight attendants) should also give "flight destination information" by telling about the country you will visit and giving pertinent missions information. (This is another place where the information in your Missions Resource File will come in handy.)

When the "plane" lands in the foreign coun-

try let the students participate in an art project about that country, enjoy a special native food (chow mein in Hong Kong or beans and rice in Mexico, etc.), meet the missionaries (played by older children or teens) and learn about their ministry, or learn a song in the language of the nation. Be sure to also include time to learn a memory verse.

Just before boarding the "plane" for the return trip home, "stamp" each passport. (The easiest way to stamp the passport is to use a children's stamp pad set and use one stamp for each nation visited, writing the name of the nation below the stamped image.) When the study series is completed, the passports provide a wonderful remembrance of the "trips" to mission fields. (If you want to be a little more elaborate, make a sticker for each nation to be pasted into the passport on completion of each "flight." To make stickers, use round labels and write or type the name of the nation visited and the memory verse on each sticker. Let the children stick the sticker into their passport as they get ready for the return "flight.")

MISSIONARY PASSPORT

The Kingdom of God

Go ye into all the world, and preach
the gospel to every creature.
Mark 16:15

26 Festive Events

Appropriate for ages 6 to 12

Teaching about missions can be made much most interesting when native foods, colorful decorations, ethnic dress and objects are used in the lesson presentations. Following are some suggestions for teaching about missions in different lands:

JAPAN:

Strip small branches of their leaves and attach pink paper flowers to simulate the Japanese cherry blossoms. Kimonos, flying fish, paper lanterns and bright-colored cushions on the floor may be used to help add atmosphere for this meeting. Serve fortune cookies in which prayer requests or Bible verses have replaced the usual fortunes.

CHINA:

Try to locate an Oriental rice cooker which may be used to hold an arrangement of flowers. Display large oriental parasols in the room.

Secure a set of Oriental rice bowls for use at the meeting. Receive the offering in one of the bowls, have one filled with prayer requests, use one to hold little rolled paper notes, each with a typed fact from the lesson, and use the fourth to hold tiny Oriental umbrellas for souvenirs for everyone to take home as a prayer or lesson reminder.

Serve Oriental cookies and tea.

INDIA:

Brass vases, pots and bells remind us of India. The vases and pots might be used in the same way as the rice bowls for China. An energetic person

might even make a tiger-skin rug for the room out of butcher paper and poster paint. Rice curry is one suggested food to serve.

AUSTRALIA:

Display boomerangs made of cardboard, toy kangaroos and koala bears on a table of greenery.

Make a large map of Australia out of strips of butcher paper taped together. Give five or six students a mission's fact about Australia. As each student presents his fact, he stands on the area of the large map he represents.

27 [Teen Volunteers]

OBJECTIVE: Practical ways teens can be missionaries right at home

Appropriate for age 11 to teens

Most Christian teens (and older children) enjoy serving the Lord by helping others, and are glad to help others if they know where the needs are. Choose an adult leader to coordinate the children's and teens' volunteer services and to serve as the go-between for individuals with special needs and the teens.

Following are some other ways children and teens can serve the Lord and develop good leadership skills:

- Teach or help with Vacation Bible School in their home church or on an Indian reservation or inner city area during the summer.
- Assist their pastor in open-air meetings, jail services and hospital visitation.
- Teens make wonderful errand runners for shut-ins, single parents, the sick and others.
- Helping in the church office provides a valuable service to the church and helps the teens develop office skills. Teens can make copies, fold bulletins, straighten up classrooms and much more.
- Nursing homes provide a wonderful place for teens to serve the Lord by reading books or letters to the elderly or by helping them with letter writing or other errands.

28 Stamps And Missions

OBJECTIVE: Interesting way to involve children in missions

Appropriate for ages 6 to 12 (and the entire congregation)

Many children and adults collect stamps. There is no better way to make the subject of missions vitally interesting than to relate it to stamp collecting. Stamps can represent people of every nation and their need for the Gospel; stamps serve as reminders that missionaries are on those fields and need our support and prayers.

Set up a trading post or stamp club so pupils can exchange stamps with one another. Appoint pupils to look up countries represented by certain stamps and report in class on missionary aspects of those countries: population, language, predominant religion, extent of missionary activities, names and addresses of missionaries in that field, etc.

Then encourage pupils to write to the missionaries or children of the missionaries, which will provide another excellent way to obtain more stamps as well as gain interesting information about the mission field.

Other ideas:

• To get your class intested in stamps and missions, order a "sampler packet" of stamps from a stamp collector supply company. Give one or more stamps to each child, and ask him to find out and report on the missionary aspects of that nation(s) at the next class meeting. (This is another place where the information collected in your Missions Resource File [see page 18] will come in handy.) At the next class, give each child a sheet of airmail stationery and the name and address of your denomination's missionary in that nation. Tell the class a bit about the missionary and ask the child who reported on that nation to write a letter to the missionary asking for more information about their field.

When the return letters start coming back from the missionaries, you can be sure your class is hooked on stamps *and* missions!

• Children also enjoy making a poster or bulletin board display of their stamps. Place a missionary's picture and name on the poster or bulletin board. Surround the picture with stamps from the country where that missionary serves. Add interesting or pertinent facts, as desired.

• Ask the stamp club members to take charge of opening exercises occasionally. At this time they can exhibit their albums and read some of the letters they have received from their missionary friends. Special prayer and an offering for these missionaries can be a part of these openings.

29 Who Am I?

OBJECTIVE: Helps children remember names and facts about missionaries

Appropriate for ages 5 through 11

After your class has learned about several missionaries (names, mission field, job, family information, etc.) have a "Who Am I?" quiz using two or three missionaries each week.

Give clues as to the missionary's identity, allowing the children time to guess between each clue. Answer with only yes or no answers. Award five points if the missionary is named on the first clue. Deduct points for each additional clue given. The first person who guesses correctly becomes "It" and gives the next clues.

Example clues:
- I am a missionary in Africa.
- I have been a missionary 14 years.
- I started five new outreach stations last year.
- I am a doctor.

30 Missionary Book Reports

OBJECTIVE: Ways to interest everyone in reading exciting missionary stories

Appropriate for ages 6 to 12 (and the entire congregation)

Provide interesting missionary books or short stories for the children to read during the week. After a child finishes a book or story, he tells the class just enough about the book to interest his friends in reading it for themselves. Each child earns a predetermined number of points for each book or story he reads, and an extra five points if he is the first to read the book or story and reports on it. (This is also excellent for women's or other adult groups.)

Another idea:

To get adults to read missionary books, ask enthusiastic persons to give short, two-minute book reviews during the worship service each Sunday for several weeks. Be sure to have several copies of each book for checking out.

31 Homemade Missions Bank

OBJECTIVE: Exciting way to bring new life to an old idea

Appropriate for ages 6 to 12

Are you met with "Ho-hum, here we go again," whenever you mention missions banks? If so, try this new, creative approach.

Challenge your students to create their own missions banks at home to be entered into a contest. Give the children an opportunity to use their own imagination, but suggest that they can use cottage-cheese cartons, margarine tubs, oatmeal containers, plastic bottles or whatever they can find that will hold money. These can be painted or covered with felt, foil, paper, Contact, cloth, wrapping paper, paper-mache or lace. They can be trimmed with rickrack, felt, lace, pompoms, buttons, seashells, tiny pine cones, seeds and sequins. Naturally the banks can have mission messages printed on them.

Give the children a deadline for bringing their banks to class. Have a contest (perhaps judged by your missionary society president and your pastor). If desired, select one winner or select banks in several categories, such as; "most beautiful," "most unique," "most 'far out' bank," etc.

Then send the banks home for the children to use to collect their offerings for the missionaries. (You might talk to the children about tithing and suggest that they contribute part of their allowance to the missionary bank at home, in addition to supporting the regular Sunday school offering.)

This project will get your missions giving off to a great start, and help maintain the enthusiasm

needed to insure that the banks arrive back in class later clinking with offerings from happy, excited children.

Another idea:

If your class is not too large, the children could be stationed outside the church door after the worship service, with banks in hand, for the adults to drop in their missionary offerings. There should be an announcement from the pulpit before this is done so the adults can be prepared.

32 Come To The Missions Fair

OBJECTIVE: Get every member of your congregation interested and involved in missions outreach

Appropriate for ages 4 to 12 (and the entire congregation)

A missions fair can be just what your church needs to get your congregation interested and excited about missions, both at home and abroad. Combining many exciting events and activities, a missions fair will appeal to everyone with its colorful displays, delicious foods, missionary guests and much more.

A missions fair involves many people and many hours of preparation, but it will be so exciting and interesting that it will inspire and encourage your entire church to a deeper commitment to missions. Mission fairs are excellent outreach opportunities too, as the entire community can be invited to participate and attend.

A missions fair can be quite simple or it can be as elaborate as you choose to make it. (For an elaborate fair, it is suggested that other churches join in the project, with each church responsible for presenting a different mission field or exhibit.)

The missions fair should be at least a two-day event taking place on Saturday and Sunday. (You could add a kick-off event on Friday night, if desired.)

Start Saturday morning with the "Tour of the Nations" during which the fair visitors will tour exhibits representing several nations. (See below.) Hold a "Worldwide Banquet" on Saturday night, featuring a guest speaker and music from around the world. If possible, serve foods representing the nations emphasized at the fair.

On Sunday morning the entire worship service should be missions-oriented. The service should feature:
* Music from the mission fields.
* Presentation of needs and prayer.
* Requests from the mission fields.
* A special missions offering.
* Pledges or faith promise emphasis.
* A missionary speaker or pastoral sermon on the "missionary call."
* An invitation to the congregation to dedicate and commit their lives to serve the Lord either on the foreign mission fields or on the home mission fields right in their own neighborhood.

For the Saturday morning "Tour of the Nations," decorate several classrooms or booths in a large auditorium to represent several different

mission field nations. Here are some suggestions for displays from various nations:

Africa: Construct a thatched hut from a large cardboard box, crepe paper and paint (teens would love making this). Display a map of Africa, pictures and facts about the missionaries and their work, and souvenirs and curios. Add some artifical palms or grasses to represent a jungle.

China, Southeast Asia: Build a brightly colored pagoda front from cardboard painted with tempera paints. Add examples of the Asian languages, clothing and foods.

South America: Arrange large plants, trees and vegetation to depict an Amazonian jungle. Add a canoe hollowed out of a log.

Alaskan Eskimo or American Indian Reservations: Build a Styrofoam block igloo, or construct a teepee from brown paper, thin poles and paint. In the teepee, display Indian handcrafts and a poster telling the needs of the Indian reservations.

Each "country" area should have samples of native foods available for the guests to enjoy. Have available at least one volunteer in each area, dressed as authentically as possible for the country he or she represents. He or she should be able to explain the artifacts and items displayed, tell missions facts and point out pictures and inter-

Continued on next page . . .

esting details about the lives and work of the missionaries on the field.

Include many photos in your displays or present separate slide presentations showing the people of each nation at work and at play.

Handouts should be available in each country's display providing information about the mission field, missionaries names and addresses, and special needs and prayer requests. Also include such information as native food recipes, a Scripture or song in the native language and other interesting information.

A very popular display is a craft area where children (and adults) can "try their hand" at making native crafts from several nations to take home. Be sure to have plenty of supplies and knowledgable helpers who know how to make the craft.

Recorded or live music, authentic to the nations represented, would be a nice addition to the "Tour of the Nations."

It is always excellent to try to involve any missionaries who are home on furlough (or retired or former missionaries) in your missions fair. They can be featured in the "Tour of the Nations" display for the country in which they serve(d), to talk with visitors and provide demonstrations of crafts, cooking, or their teaching methods with the natives, etc.

Preparation for the Missions Fair must begin at least six months before the event in order to have a smooth running event.

Here is a checklist of things you will need to do or have for your Missions Fair to be a success:

• Make contact with your denomination headquarters six months in advance of the fair to arrange for missionaries to be present as guests or speakers at the fair. (If active missionaries are not available, many retired of former missionaries would be happy to share their experiences with your group.)

• Choose a facility with several individual classrooms or one large auditorium that has space for several separate exhibits for the "Tour of the Nations."

• Form a planning committee made up of people from all areas (and churches, if several churches are planning a fair together) which will be involved. This committee with be responsible for planning and coordinating the entire event.

(This is a good time to involve members of your women's missionary society and missions clubs [See page 25] in helping with the many coordinational details of the fair.)

• Prepare and obtain pastoral or board and committee approval of financial goals and budgets.

• Prepare publicity announcements, including news releases for radio, TV and newspapers, and posters for local display.

• Obtain or prepare decorations, handouts, craft items and other materials.

• Decide on foods to be served and make arrangements for refreshments, food service and banquet. Order supplies.

• Prepare programs and song sheets and have printed.

• Schedule music and musicians.

• Arrange for use, set-up and operation of all needed audio-visual equipment and obtain needed slides, filmstrips, records, etc. Be sure equipment is properly set-up and in working order the day before the fair is to begin.

Don't be discouraged by the multitude of details involved in planning and preparing your Missions Fair. It is sure to be a highpoint of your church year and will bring new life to every missionary endeavor in which your church is involved.

33 Music Of The World

OBJECTIVE: Delightful way to listen and learn about missions

Appropriate for age 8 to teens (and the entire congregation)

Plan a special evening of music from around the world performed by the soloists, bands and singing groups in your church. For a really gala event, join with other churches and include an orchestra and large choir. The repertoire should include a variety of music styles from around the world including Christian songs and hymns, folk songs, classical compositions, children's songs and more.

If there are any foreign exchange students available who could sing or play their native music, it would add greatly to the program and make the students feel at home. You may also find others in your community who can contribute native music to the event. Encourage participants to wear authentic national costumes, if possible.

Pictures from the mission fields can be placed around the auditorium for decorations or slides from the different countries can be shown as background for the musical presentations.

Be sure to present a missions challenge for a specific project and collect an offering.

Another idea:

This musical evening could be organized as a fund raiser by including outstanding local musicians on the program and charging an admission fee which would be donated to the missions project.

34 | **Globe Banks**

OBJECTIVE: Develops the habit of giving to missions

Appropriate for ages 6 to 12

Every class should have a globe bank or some other type of bank in which to collect money for missions. Talk to the children about giving to missions and ask them to place their offerings in the missions bank before class begins. (Emphasize to the children to give to both the regular offering as well as the missionary offering each week. It is also wise to send a note home to explain to the parents about the missionary offering in your class.)

Discuss with the children various ways in which their offerings can be used by the missionaries. (They should know that because they give, the missionary can use his time to work for God instead of having to earn money for food, shelter and clothes. Sometimes their money will help meet an emergency need on the mission field, help to build a church for people who do not have one, or help to provide food and clothing for children who don't have parents.)

Help the children choose where their missionary offering will be used or pick something to buy for the mission field with the money they have given. This helps develop in the children the habit and desire of giving regularly to missions. Also help the children participate in deciding their offering amount goal for the quarter or year. Guide them in determining this amount so that it will not be too easily attainable yet, will be within their reach.

Help the children understand how their

money reaches the missionaries, including every step through which the money goes from your class until it reaches the missionary.

Keep the missionary bank in the same place each week, and let the children take turns counting the offering after class. The children's interest will mount as their progress is visualized on a "giving chart" which shows the amount they have given.

35 Recycling For Missions

OBJECTIVE: Easy way to help missions and the ecology of our land

Appropriate for age 6 to teens

Plan a special springtime outing for your class or all children and teens in your church. In advance, choose an area littered with trash. (Check local or state laws regarding picking up trash along road or highway ditches.) Also investigate what types of recycling plants are in your area and check with them to determine what they will accept.

Provide large trash bags and divide the children into pairs. Each pair should collect either soda and pop cans, glass bottles, or other trash (so the refuse does not have to be sorted for recycling). It is well to provide lightweight plastic gloves (surgical type) for the children to wear while picking up the trash. Be sure the group is adequately chapperoned.

Spend the morning picking up trash, then break for a picnic lunch. Be sure the children either wash their hands or clean them with pre-moistened wipes before eating.

After lunch, haul the collected refuse to your recyling plant and let the children help unload it. The money received for the items can be used for a missions project.

36 Art Display

OBJECTIVE: Children make crafts authentic to the mission fields

Appropriate for ages 6 to 12

Children enjoy using their hands to make things, so lessons reinforced with related craft projects are often remembered longest. In conjunction with missionary study, children can make attractive crafts authentic to the culture and country being studied.

Instructions for three easy crafts, from Mexico or Central America, Japan and Alaska, are found below. Or select a craft from the country you are studying which the students can duplicate with locally available materials.

Other ideas:

* Hold a special "International Craft Fair" depicting the arts and crafts of various countries where your missionaries are at work. Display authentic arts and crafts from these nations, plus crafts made by your students. (An attractive display to include also is the Relief Map and Table-top Village on page 19.)
* Space and materials could be given to let attendees use their talents to "try their hand" at duplicating some crafts. Provide index cards listing the craft's country of origin, missionaries' names and a prayer request to take home along with the completed craft.

Mexican Pottery:

Mix self-hardening modeling clay from the recipe below. Work with it until it forms easily, then shape it into one of the pottery shapes pictured (or a shape of the potter's choice). After the clay hardens, paint the pottery with tempera paint in bright colors. After the paint is dry, more intricate designs can either be painted on with a brush or drawn on with markers.

> Self-hardening Modeling Clay
> 1 cup flour
> 1 cup salt
> Water to mix

Mix the flour and salt with enough water to make the mixture creamy. Do not heat. Place on a solid surface and knead, then form into pottery shapes as desired. The mixture will harden and set. When dry, it can be painted.

Japanese Laquered Box:

Paint a box (similar to a school box or a corsage box) with black gloss enamel. Crush several egg shells into small pieces. (Egg shells may be colored with Easter egg dye first, if desired.)

When the black paint is dry, use tweezers to pick up the egg shell pieces to arrange into a floral design on the box top. Put a tiny drop of glue on the underside of each egg shell piece or carefully paint a thin coat of clear varnish over the box top so the pieces will stick.

When you have completed the design, spread a coat of clear varnish over the entire surface of the box top and allow to dry. You now have a work of art like that made by Japanese art masters.

Indian Totem Pole:

Turn old shoe boxes into unique totem poles, (you do not need the box tops). Paint or draw faces and other features on the bottoms and sides of the boxes using tempera paints or felt-tip markers. Use construction paper or poster board to make wings, ears, or beaks to glue onto the boxes. Stack the boxes end-to-end and glue or staple them together to construct the totem poles.

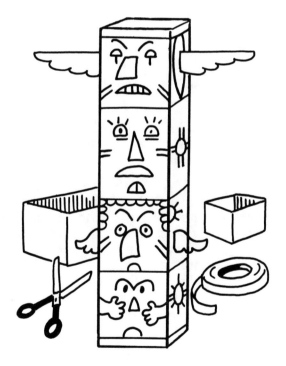

37 Be A Missionary

OBJECTIVE: Shows children how they can be missionaries

Appropriate for ages 6 to 12

These practical missions lessons help the children understand that they can be missionaries by giving, praying, and telling others about Jesus. All three segments below can be used in one class or over three separate classes. Suggested memory verses are listed in each segment.

For "Be a Missionary by Going," make a big green GO sign from a large piece of poster board. For "Be a Missionary by Praying" draw a large silhouette of a child in prayer on poster board. For "Be a Missionary by Giving," draw a simple outline of a bank building on a sheet of posterboard.

Cut the other pictures indicated with the readings out of magazines or coloring books. Duplicate this page and cut each short reading apart and give one to each child to read in numbered sequence. As he reads his part, the child holds up the corresponding picture then attaches his picture to the bulletin board near the large sign or poster. Allow time to discuss each reading, if desired. The paragraphs to be read may be glued or taped to the backs of the corresponding pictures.

BE A MISSIONARY BY GOING
Go ye into all the world, and preach the gospel.
(Mark 16:15)

Go (#1)
(A child holds up the GO sign, then tacks it to the bulletin board.) The Bible tells us to go and tell others about Jesus. Missionaries go all over the world telling others about Jesus. Some of us may become missionaries and have the chance to go all over the world to tell others about Jesus. But even if we don't, there are places we go every day where we can be missionaries.

School (#2)
Many boys and girls at school have never heard about Jesus. We can tell them about Him. We can invite them to come to our church to hear about Him. We can GO to school and be missionaries for Jesus.

Home (#3)
Sometimes there are people living in our own homes who do not know about Jesus. We can tell them about Him. We can invite them to come to church to hear about Him. We can GO home and be missionaries there for Jesus.

Playing Child (#4)
Some of the boys and girls we play with in our neighborhood may not know about Jesus. We can tell them about Him. We can invite them to come to church to hear about Him. We can GO around our neighborhood while we play, and be missionaries for Jesus.

Church (#5)
When boys and girls come to church someone must tell them about Jesus. When we do our parts at church we are helping to tell about Jesus. We can GO to church and be missionaries for Jesus.

BE A MISSIONARY BY GIVING
Give, and it shall be given to you;
(Luke 6:38)

Bank Building(#1)
(A child holds up the poster of the bank building, then tacks it to the bulletin board.) The Bible tells us to GIVE to Jesus. When we give to Jesus we are obeying God's Word. When we give here on earth it is just as if we are making deposits in the Bank of Heaven. When we go there we will be able to be as rich as our deposits made us. If we have deposited a lot, we will have a lot. If we have deposited a little bit, that is what we will have.

Money (#2)

(Use "play" money or real dollar bill.) The first thing we think of giving is money. Most people have some money, even if it is only a penny or two. When we give money, God uses it to tell others about Jesus. He uses every penny. We can deposit our money in the Bank of Heaven when we GIVE it to Jesus.

BE A MISSIONARY BY PRAYING

"Pray without ceasing.
(1 Thessalonians 5:17)

Praying Child (#1)

(A child holds up the poster of the praying child, then tacks it to the bulletin board.) Each morning when we first get up is a good time to PRAY. We can pray that God will take care of us all day. We can pray that He will help us to tell others about Jesus. We can ask Him to take care of the missionaries who are telling others about Jesus all over the world.

Bright Sun (#2)

All day long we talk to God. Sometimes we might think of something we want to tell Him while we are walking along the sidewalk. We can pray to Him right then, without even closing our eyes.

Moon (#3)

Each evening before we go to bed we can talk to God. We can thank Him for the day He has given us and for taking care of us. We can ask Him to take care of the missionaries who are telling others about Jesus all over the world. We can pray for our mothers and our father and families. We can thank Him for a time of rest.

38 ┃ Prayer Wheel

OBJECTIVE: Inspires children to pray for missionaries

Appropriate for ages 8 to 12

Duplicate the two circles of the Missionary Prayer Wheel on pages 49 and 50 for each child. Prior to class glue each circle onto tagboard or lightweight cardboard and allow to dry. (If you have access to a copy machine which can copy onto lightweight card stock, you can eliminate the need to glue the wheels to tagboard.) Before class, the teacher or another adult should carefully cut out the wedge-shaped window on the first circle using a craft knife. Punch a hole in the center of each circle.

In class, give each child one of each of the circles. Give the children time to cut them out, and color them, if desired. Show the children how to put their wheel together, (see illustration) so the circle with the cut-out window is on top, and fasten with a paper fastener. Tape down the prongs of the paper fastener to prevent scratching.

Show the children how to use their Missionary Prayer Wheel to pray for the missionaries and people of a different continent and to learn Bible verses about missions. In class, each week for six weeks, discuss a different continent, have special prayer and learn the memory verse. Let the children take their Prayer Wheels home to remind them to pray for the missionaries and people of each continent.

Other ideas:
- Using a copy machine with enlarging capa-

bilities, enlarge the two circles to make a giant prayer wheel for use in the classroom during the six weeks you study the continents and learn the memory verse.
- Let the children use their Missionary Prayer Wheel for personal prayer and memorization. Award a small prize to the first child who is able to correctly recite all six memory verses.

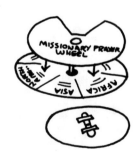

Missionary Prayer Wheel

The Lord . . . is not willing
that any should perish,
but that all should come
to repentance.
2 Peter 3:9

Continued on next page . . .

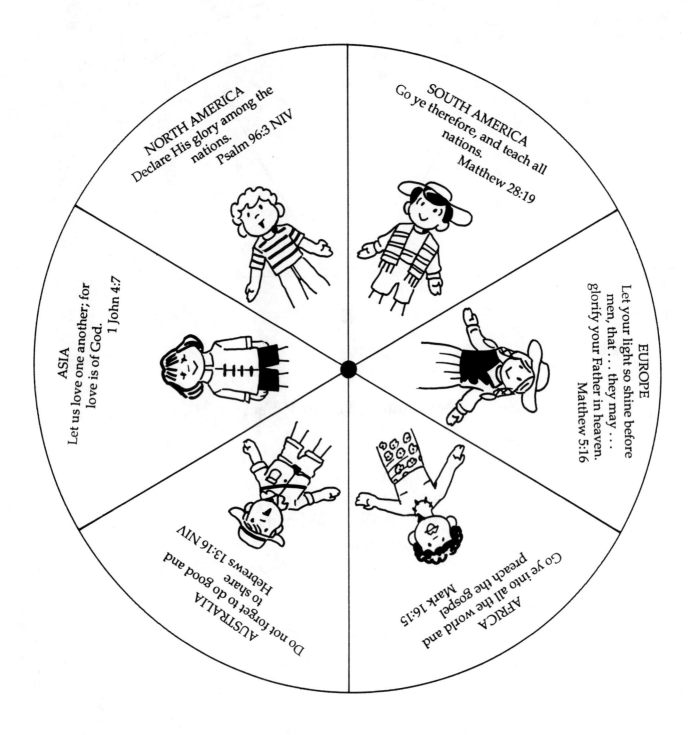

39 Worship Themes

OBJECTIVE: Bible studies on God's call to spread the Gospel

Appropriate for age 10 to teens

Build missionary study programs and devotionals around themes which will emphasize the scriptural basis of God's call to serve Him and spread the Gospel.

Following are three different Bible study suggestions, each containing Scriptures which are to be read and/or discussed with your students or Bible study members:

Obeying God's call:

O	bey	Joshua 24:24
B	elieve	Acts 16:31
E	ndure	1 Corinthians 13:7
Y	ield	2 Chronicles 30:8
I	ncline	Joshua 24:23
N	igh	Psalm 145:18
G	ive	Deuteronomy 15:10
G	o	Mark 16:15
O	bserve	Psalm 107:43
D	eclare	Psalm 96:3
S	eek	Matthew 6:33
C	ommit	Psalm 37:5
A	bide	John 15:10
L	ove	1 John 4:18
L	abor	1 Corinthians 15:58

People God called to serve:

Paul's message	1 Thessalonians 2:12
Samuel's call	1 Samuel 3:4
Levi called	Mark 2:14
Call of Amos	Amos 7:14, 15
Christ's call to us	John 15:16
Our mandate	1 Peter 5:10

Ways we let our light shine:

Prayer life	Proverbs 15:8
Devotions	Colossians 3:16
Thanksgiving	Psalm 69:30
Honesty	Romans 13:13
Brotherly love	1 John 4:7, 8
Good for evil	Romans 12:20, 21
Benevolence	James 1:27
Fellowship	1 John 1:1

40 | Mother/Daughter Banquet

OBJECTIVE: Builds understanding of what it would be like to live in a foreign nation

Appropriate for mothers and daughters age 10 and older

Use the theme "Mothers Around the World" for a very special mother/daughter banquet. Decorate the banquet tables with dolls from around the world.

Arrange in advance for several mothers and their daughters to tell about family customs in various countries. Include such information as how women dress, how household chores are different and how foods are prepared and eaten.

If your guests will include women who have recently immigrated to the U.S., ask them to tell about their native country and wear their native dress. (You might consider inviting immigrant women from the community to speak and as an opportunity to get acquainted and invite them to your church.)

Include missions information and prayer for the countries profiled.

Be sure to encourage "adopted" mothers and daughters so all women and girls may participate, regardless of family situation.

Another idea:

This concept could also be adapted for a father/son banquet. Decorations could be along a safari motif with pictures (or taxidermy specimens if available) of wildlife of the various nations displayed.

41 "Share A Spare" For Missions

OBJECTIVE: A fun alternative for Halloween Trick or Treat to help missions

Appropriate for ages 8 to 14

It's still possible for your class to have fun without the negative connotations of Halloween and Trick or Treat, while keeping the missionaries or needy people at the same time.

Gather your class and go from house to house. (Be sure each group of children is chaperoned.) After knocking and waiting for a response, the children say, "Share a Spare for Missions." The children should then explain to the resident that they are from your church (give the name and location), that they are collecting items for the homeless, an orphanage, rescue mission, or specific mission field, and that rather than receiving candy for themselves, they would like to have an item for the orphanage (or whatever).

Have a suggested list of items you want to collect (and items of which people are likely to have a "spare") such as a bar of soap, towel, washcloth, box of crayons, baby layette items, or canned goods (if for home missions).

Thank the person heartily for their contribution and leave a Halloween or other soul-winning tract whether the person contributed or not. (Halloween tracts are available from the American Tract Society, Box 462008, Garland, Texas 75046-2008.)

It is well to advertise this project around the community before Halloween so that residents will have knowledge of what the children will be doing. (You may feel more comfortable with the children visiting the homes of congregation members and friends rather than the general public. If so, promote the outreach heavily within

your church for two or three weeks before Halloween.)

Since "dressing up" is a big part of the fun, you may wish to allow the children to dress up as people of foreign lands or as missionaries in working clothes, but discourage the traditional Halloween costumes of ghosts and witches, etc.

When the "Share a Spare" collecting is done, the children may return to the church for a party with games and refreshments and help sort out the items collected to be sent to the mission field or to people in need.

42 Thanksgiving Offering

OBJECTIVE: Unique way to gather a special Thanksgiving offering

Appropriate for ages 6 to 12 (and the entire congregation)

Prepare a large cornucopia or horn of plenty from chicken wire and papier-mâché. Paint it and fill with real or artificial fruit, vegetables and grains. Display in a prominent place in the church. (If the entire congregation is involved, it is preferable to display the cornucopia at the front of the sanctuary.)

Make a public announcement regarding the special Thanksgiving missionary offering several weeks in advance and then distribute a piece of plastic fruit with a slit cut in the top to each member or family. The plastic fruit is to be filled with coins over the following weeks and then brought back to church for the special Thanksgiving service when the fruit will be placed in the horn of plenty.

43 Christmas Greeting Card Offering

OBJECTIVE: Innovative way of raising money for missions

Appropriate for age 10 to 12

At Christmas, instead of exchanging greeting cards wth other members of your church congregation, ask each individual or family to donate the money which is saved in cards and postage to the special Christmas missionary project, then sign their greetings on a giant Christmas card displayed in the church foyer.

The giant "card" may be made by decorating a large poster board with Christmas greetings, leaving plenty of room for people to sign their names. Have a box or collection container near the giant card so families can leave their offering of the money saved by not sending individual cards.

44 | A Caroling We Will Go

OBJECTIVE: Reach the neighborhood with the Gospel at Christmas time

Appropriate for age 10 to teens

The Christmas season provides opportunities for reaching your neighborhood with the Gospel while your class has a good time too.

Take your class caroling at homes in the neighborhood. After you have finished singing, leave Gospel tracts with the residents. Contact your denomination headquarters for a listing of tracts they have available for you to order, or order Christmas tracts from the American Tract Society, Box 462008, Garland, Texas 75046-2008.

---

45 | Christmas Drama

OBJECTIVE: Show how Christmas is celebrated around the world

Appropriate for age 8 to teens (and the entire congregation)

Using books at the library or letters from missionaries or other sources, learn about Christmas customs in various nations. For a special Christmas program, involve your children, teens and adults in pantomiming or acting out some of these customs, accompanied by appropriate music and costumes.

Then tell about your missionaries in these countries and their needs. Collect an offering, and conclude the evening with refreshments of authentic Christmas foods from the countries profiled.

46 A Country Each Year

OBJECTIVE: Develop in-depth interest and understanding of a specific nation

Appropriate for age 8 to teens (and the entire congregation)

You may choose to concentrate your missionary focus all year on one mission field. Here are some ways to build a deep love and spiritual bond between the people of your church, the missionaries in that nation, and its people:

- Study the culture, dress, food, literature, history, religion, geography, customs, games, etc. of that nation.
- Become intimately acquainted with the missionary families by "adopting" them (see page 9) and learning about their work, their hobbies, special needs, concerns, blessings and praises. Pray for them daily.
- Keep scrapbooks about the nation and mission work there.
- Collect native clothing from the nation and wear to special events.
- Make a pledge or faith promise for support of missions in that country.
- Hold a dinner with foods from that country served.
- Learn how to write and speak and read a bit of the language of the nation.
- Show films and slides about the nation.
- Have a special speaker who has visited the nation or is an expert on some aspect of the

nation.
- Plan a drama or pageant about that country.
- Use many of the other ideas in this book to round out your missionary emphasis.

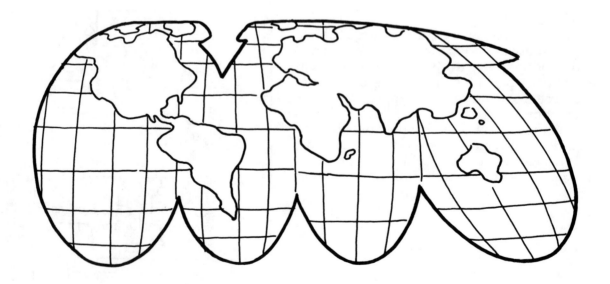

47 A Missionary Is ... Devotional

OBJECTIVE: Biblical characteristics of a missionary and how we can be missionaries wherever we are

Appropriate for age 10 to teens

The Lord has called each of us to spread the Gospel around the world. This devotional shares the Biblical qualities of a missionary and challenges us all to be missionaries wherever we go.

• A Missionary is A SENT ONE — Read John 20:21 and Mark 16:15.

God sent Jesus to earth to show His love for us and to die so every person can accept the free gift of eternal life. Jesus told His disciples that they too were sent to minister to the world and to preach the Good News to every person. A missionary is anyone who obeys this command and goes to share the Gospel with people who need love and who need Christ. A missionary goes in answer to the call and command of God.

You are a missionary too. With whom have you shared the Gospel?

• A missionary is A LENT ONE — Read Acts 13:1-4.

Missionaries are usually greatly loved by relatives, friends, and home church people. Missionaries are usually hard workers who have plenty of things to do and who willingly serve the church at home. But when God calls someone to the mission field, his family, friends and church LEND him to the Lord to serve others. It is then their responsibility to pray for him and support him.

You are a missionary too. To whom have you LENT yourself in service to the Lord?

• A missionary is A BENT ONE — Read Ephesians 6:18-20 and Philippians 4:6-7.

Each missionary must have God's help to carry out the work of the Lord, or he will fail. The missionary will face problems and dangers, which could cause worry and fear and lead to failure. It is through prayer that the missionary gets the wisdom and God's power to solve the problems, to win others to Christ, and to have peace even in the midst of danger.

You are a missionary too. Are you regularly BENT in prayer, asking the Lord to guide your life as you serve Him?

• A missionary is A SPENT ONE — Read 2 Corinthians 12:9-10; 2 Corinthians 7:5-6; and Philippians 3:10.

The person who gives himself completely to God and His work will sometimes become tired. Missionaries must trust God to care for them in countries where there are many diseases, unfamiliar foods and dangers. They must be willing to give themselves totally to the Lord for His work, knowing that God promises His children a glorious reward in Heaven.

You are a missionary too? When was the last time you were tired because your were working hard for the Lord?

(Close the devotional with a prayer of consecration, asking the audience to personally dedicate their lives to serve the Lord as His missionaries, either at home or abroad.)

48 — Prayer-A-Day

OBJECTIVE: Involve each member of your church family in daily prayer for missions

Appropriate for age 6 to adults

Missionaries are human beings like ourselves who struggle with the same weaknesses we do—the limitations of our human bodies, spiritual weakness, and the loneliness and longings of the human heart. They need much prayer so they may experience God's presence and receive His power to carry out the work to which He has called them. Try the ideas which follow to encourage every member of your church family to pray daily for at least one missionary family:

PRAYER CALENDAR:
(For all ages)

Reproduce the calendar grid on page 59. Fill in the correct month, and write in the dates in the correct squares. If desired, write specific prayer requests (or missions-related events) in some of the daily blocks. Place a picture of a missionary or missionary family in the box and write in their names, mission field address and special needs. Distribute to all.

For use with children, show how to use the calendar to remind them to pray for the missionary family each day. (See World Time Chart on pages 16 and 17 for ways to help the children pray for different needs and at different times of the day.) Each day, when the the child has completed his prayer, he can color in the space for that day on his calendar.

FAMILY PRAYER BOX
(For all ages)

Decorate an ordinary recipe box (3 by 5 inch size) with pictures of missionaries or a collage map of various countries of the world. Create

several missionary prayer cards to go in each box and give one box to each family who has committed to pray for missionaries each day. Cards should include information about different missionaries: their names and address, occupation (doctor, teacher, pilot, etc.) and their special personal needs or needs of the field. Include a picture if possible. Your church families may read and choose one missionary or missionary family each day to pray for.

Each week, make one new card to give to each of your church families to take home to add to their Family Prayer Box.

Missionary Prayer Calendar _____, 19 ___

I thank my God upon every remembrance of you, always in every prayer . . . making request for you. Philippians 1:3-4 NKJV

Sunday	Monday	Tuesday	Wednesday	Thursday	Friday	Saturday

This month, pray for:

Names

Address

Special Prayer Needs:

49 Living For Jesus

OBJECTIVE: Helps children and teens choose ways they can serve the Lord

Appropriate for age 6 to teens

Duplicate the "Living For Jesus" activity sheet on page 61 for each student.

Before distributing the sheet, talk to the class about how they can serve Jesus and live for Him. How can they obey Jesus' command to "preach the Gospel" and tell others about Him?

Ask if any children would like to ask Jesus to be their friend and become a part of God's family. In addition, you might ask if any children would like to give their lives to Jesus completely to do whatever He asks. If so, take these children aside to show them the plan of salvation from the Bible and pray with them while an assistant continues with the class. Guide the children who want to dedicate their lives also. (If the majority of the class responds simply lead the entire class through the plan of salvation and work individually with the children who want to dedicate their lives to Jesus.)

Distribute the activity sheet and explain the instructions. Talk about how each of the activities is serving the Lord and telling someone about Jesus. Ask the children to name other ways they could do this.

When the children have completed the worksheet, ask if anyone would like to share with the

rest of the class what they think God would like them to do. Then ask the class to join in praying for that student. Close the class by singing a song or hymn of dedication the children know, and prayer.

LIVING FOR JESUS

God has a special job for each Christian to do for Him. Read Acts 13:1-5 and find out how the Holy Spirit gave two men their work to do.

Now think about yourself for a moment. If you belong to Jesus Christ, God has something for YOU to do.

Here are some suggestions. Stop and ask the Lord what He wants you to do, and then mark with an X the items you think God wants you to do. Write in additional things if they are not listed here.

_____ Bring someone new to Sunday school

_____ Give more help to your mother or father

_____ Set a good example to others in your class at school

_____ Pray daily for your pastor and a missionary

_____ Give some of your allowance to Jesus

_____ Tell a friend that Jesus loves them

_____

_____

Pray this prayer to ask Jesus to help you do the things you chose:

Dear Jesus,
   Thank You for being my Friend and making me a part of God's family. Please help me to do what You want me to do and to help tell other people about You. In Jesus' Name, Amen.

Present your bodies a living sacrifice...unto God . . .
Romans 12:1

50 Meeting Christ

Appropriate for any age

Teachers (and all Christians) need to be sensitive to the spiritual needs of their students (and the people around them). Make evangelism the keynote of each class (and the goal of every activity). Each lesson should be a step in accomplishing the goal of leading each person to Jesus.

Follow these basic steps in helping your students accept Jesus as their Savior and then grow as Christians: (It is easier for most young children to understand he becomes a member of God's family.)

1. Explain simply to the children how to ask Jesus Christ to become their personal Savior. Show your students what God says in His Word:
   a. God loves you so much that He wants you to be with Him now and always (John 3:16).
   b. Those who do wrong do not please God, for God is perfect and holy. God's word for wrong doing is sin. God says you have sinned (Romans 3:23), sin will destroy your life and your sin must be punished (Romans 6:23).
   c. God loves you so much He sent His Son, the Lord Jesus Christ to die on the cross (1 Corinthians 15:3) so your sins can be forgiven.
   d. When you are really sorry you have sinned, you want to stop doing wrong and believe Jesus Christ died on the cross for your sin. Then God forgives you. You become a member of God's family (John 1:12) because Christ is your Savior.
2. After a student in simple faith trusts Christ and believes that Jesus took the punishment for his sin, encourage him to thank God in his own words that Jesus died for him and has

forgiven him.
3. To help the children grow as Christians, explain that when a Christian sins, he should tell God of the sin and ask God to forgive him in Jesus' name (1 John 1:9).
4. Encourage the student to tell others that he trusts Jesus Christ as his Savior and has become a Christian.
5. Explain to the student that he may grow spiritually by:
   a. Reading the Bible — Psalm 119:11
   b. Praying — Philippians 4:6
   c. Obeying God — James 1:22

Be prepared to give the young Christian spiritual help and encouragement. Pray for him. Give his name to your pastor so that a call can be made in his home as soon as possible.

51 Last Cent Offering

OBJECTIVE: A simple and painless way to gather extra change for missions

Appropriate for age 6 to teens (and the entire congregation)

Label a gallon jar "GIVE YOUR LAST CENTS TO MISSIONS" and glue several coins on the outside of the jar. Cut a slit in the lid.

Announce in your classroom or department, or from the pulpit that at the close of each Sunday morning service, the jar is placed in a prominent location where people will pass by and can give the last cent in their pockets or purses to missions.

52 Missionary Benediction

OBJECTIVE: Inspirational closing for any missionary event

Appropriate for age 10 to teens (and the entire congregation)

Use this scriptural benediction at the close of your missionary study meetings or any missionary event:

May God be gracious to us and bless us and make His face shine upon us; may Your ways be known on earth, Your salvation among all nations.

Psalm 67:1-2 (NIV)